D0605249

PENNSYLVANIA
LAND OF MANY DREAMS

The publishers wish to thank The Pennsylvania Historical and Museum Commission for permission to photograph their premises at Pennsbury Manor, and The Bucks County Historical Society for providing facilities at Fonthill and The Mercer Museum.

First published in England 1984 by Colour Library Books Ltd.
© 1984 Illustrations and text: Colour Library Books Ltd.,
   Guildford, Surrey, England.
Display and text filmsetting by Acesetters Ltd.,
   Richmond, Surrey, England.
Colour separations by Llovet S.A., Barcelona, Spain.
Printed and bound in Barcelona, Spain by Rieusset and Eurobinder.
All rights reserved.
Published 1984 by Crescent Books, distributed by Crown Publishers, Inc.
Printed in Spain.
ISBN 0 517 440989
h g f e d c b a

PENNSYLVANIA

LAND OF MANY DREAMS

Text by Bill Harris

Featuring the photography of
NEIL SUTHERLAND

Produced by
TED SMART and DAVID GIBBON

CRESCENT BOOKS
NEW YORK

Every year at the crack of dawn on February 2, a group of very serious gentlemen dressed in formal clothes gathers on a hillside just outside Punxutawney, Pennsylvania, to watch for a woodchuck.

The occasion is Groundhog Day and the beast is no less a creature than Punxutawney Phil, America's official groundhog. If Phil sees his shadow when he comes out that morning, he goes back into hibernation, because it's a sign to one and all that winter will last another six weeks.

According to tradition, Phil is a much more reliable forecaster than the National Weather Service and word is flashed from coast to coast when he pokes his head out from his burrow.

No matter what people think of Punxutawney Phil, the event sets people as far away as Puyallup, Washington, to thinking that Pennsylvania has some pretty funny place names.

Punxutawney isn't very far from Smicksburg, but Pennsylvania can do better than that. Hollsopple, for instance; or Wilmerding, Hop Bottom or Wapwallopen. There once was a city in Lehigh County called Sideropolis, but the city fathers thought that was too pretentious, so they changed it to Catasaqua. No one in Catawissa raised an eyebrow. Neither town is far from another that changed its name to honor a local boy who made good, Jim Thorpe. When the future football star learned how to play the game, his home town was called Mauch Chunk. What other state can boast having post offices in places named Shickshinny or Loyalsock, Normalville or Neshaming? Does mail destined for Nanty Glo ever get misdirected to Nanticoke? And what do you suppose goes on behind closed doors in Cheat Haven?

A creek that winds its way through Berks County has always been known as Maiden Creek, even before the town of Virginville was established on its banks. It's not far from Sinking Springs.

Puzzletown, Applevold and Forty Fort, are all names that make you want to stop and read the signs the state has placed along the roadside explaining where and how such names originated. The list is nearly endless. There are more than 15,000 place names crammed into the state's 45,000 square miles. It's not hard to find Warrior Run, Dirtycamp Run or Paw Paw Run, but if you're looking for Dry Run you may be in trouble: there are 16 different ones! There are 49 Laurel Runs but, after all, mountain laurel is the official state flower. But there is only one Lower Gum Stump, a single Sober and one solitary Bird-in-Hand.

No tourist ever goes to Pennsylvania Dutch country without mailing back a postcard from Intercourse. It's the thing to do. Climax and Desire often provide photographs worth smirking over, but Decorum is a place tourists often miss.

If Pennsylvania gave the country some of its most interesting place names (the name of the State of Wyoming, taken west by white men, comes from the Algonquin Indians who first named Pennsylvania's Wyoming Valley), it has also added some words to the American vocabulary.

Call someone a "punk" and you have Pennsylvania to thank for your choice of word. It's an Indian word that means "rotten wood." It entered the English language as a description of a certain type of person during the Homestead steel strike in 1892, when the mill owners brought in Pinkerton guards to knock some heads together. They were always called "Pinks," but the strikers changed it slightly, picking up the local word for rotten.

If you call a supermarket a grocery store, you're using the Pennsylvania word for it. And if you call a cigar a "stogy," you're going back to the days when Pennsylvania provided the Conestoga Wagons that took the country west.

Pennsylvania gave us the Philadelphia lawyer back in 1735, when newspaper editor John Peter Zenger went on trial in New York to defend the rights of a free press. The man who defended him was Philadelphian Andrew Hamilton. And if you think it was the Indians who first called corn "maize," you may be surprised to know that the word was introduced into the language by Pennsylvania's William Penn.

Of all the men who had a part in America's history, the one who gave us most of the ideals we claim to live by was this man William Penn.

His father was an Admiral in the British Navy. In 1661, when the monarchy was restored, the elder Penn commanded the ship that carried Charles II back home in triumph. In return, the King granted him a knighthood and the two became close friends.

The friendship represented an opportunity for the Admiral, who wanted his son to have a career in politics. But, as young men often do, William Penn had dreams of his own. He wanted to be a soldier.

He became one, and a good one, too. But then fate stepped in when he met some Quakers in Ireland. He went to their meetings and eventually joined them.

William Penn had always had strong feelings against persecution, which was common in 17th-century England. When he became a Quaker he joined the most persecuted group there was. Among other indignities, England had a law specifically forbidding more than five Quakers to gather together at any one time "under the pretext of worship." As the prominent son of a prominent man, his decision to become one of the hated Quakers made him a convenient target. In 1668 he was arrested and taken to the Tower of London to think things over. But time to think was just what Penn needed and, as often happens with imprisoned revolutionary thinkers, the young man devised a plan for the future.

Penn called his plan a "holy experiment." Its future would blossom in a place he called "Philadelphia," but he didn't know then where Philadelphia would be.

When he wasn't thinking about his holy experiment, he put his mind to the problem of getting out of the Tower with his head still attached to his body. To that end he wrote a pamphlet pleading his own case. When the King read it, he ordered Penn released.

Now, any ordinary man who crossed the drawbridge of the Tower of London going out would probably make it a point never to cross it going the other way again. But nobody ever suggested that William Penn was an ordinary man. The first thing he did when he got his freedom was to go to work to gain freedom for other Quakers still in prison. He went back to prison himself for his trouble.

When he came to trial Penn pleaded his own case. He did it so brilliantly that the jury, though few of them had any sympathy for Quakers, found him not guilty. The judge was furious. He had to set William free, but ordered all 12 jurors thrown into jail for contempt of court.

Penn took it on himself to defend them and took their case to the highest court in England, where the Lord Chief Justice ruled that members of a jury may never be punished for a verdict. The decision still stands as a basic part of common law both in England and in the United States.

Ten years later, Penn decided it was time to get on with the holy experiment and he went to the King for a grant of land in North America. On March 4, 1681, the King signed a charter that gave Penn more than 28 million acres of territory. It made him the largest single landowner, except for the King himself, in the entire British Empire. William Penn was 36 years old at the time.

King Charles suggested that they call the territory "Penn," in honor of his friend the Admiral. But William Penn thought it the height of vanity, and unseemly for a Quaker, to name the colony after his family. Besides, it didn't have a catchy ring to it. He countered with a suggestion that they name the place "New Wales." The Penn family's roots were in Wales and the countryside they were naming resembled Wales more than any other part of the British Isles. The King rejected that idea, so Penn came back with the name "Sylvania," a fancy name for woodland. The King nodded his head in agreement and then began to smile to himself. The

monarch took his quill and added the letters P-E-N-N to the front of the name, then unceremoniously waved the young man away. The discussion was over.

Penn was upset at having lost his case, but later he told friends that the word "penn" in Welsh means "head" and that the name Pennsylvania really meant "high woodlands." But generations of schoolchildren have since been taught that it means Penn's woodlands, and the idea of egoism on the part of William Penn has never entered their minds.

The woodlands were alive with color when William Penn arrived for the first time, in 1682. It was late October, still the best time of the year in the Northeast. But he wasn't there to admire the countryside. There was work to be done; not least finding the right spot for the city that would be the centerpiece of his new colony. He had already given it a name, of course. It was the same name as that of one of the early Christian cities in Asia Minor which, when translated, means "City of Brotherly Love." It had been taken by a religious group in England, whose beliefs were similar to those of the Quakers, for an ideal community they had hoped to establish. Penn borrowed the name from them because it suited perfectly the ideal community he had in mind.

The spot he picked, on the banks of the Delaware River, had a small harbor and a beach. The land around it was high enough to provide a perfect place for a city and William Penn had a perfect city in mind. What he wanted, he said, was a "green country town."

In his travels he had seen the great cities of Europe and hadn't always liked what he saw. He was also well aware of the cities that had already been established in the New World and knew they were growing without a plan. His new city would have a plan for growth and that, he was convinced, would make it one of the great cities of the world.

For openers, he ordered that Philadelphia would have no crooked streets. They would all be straight and wide and they would all lead to the river. He told his surveyors that he also wanted the roads to lead out of the city, so that it would be convenient to reach other cities yet unbuilt. He pointed out that new streets would eventually have to be added and ordered that space be left for them before any land was sold for building. He specified that no houses could be built within 200 paces of the harbor so there would be plenty of room for a future commercial center. And he asked that home builders center their structures on building lots "...so there may be ground on each side for gardens, orchards or field, that it may be a green country town which will never be burnt and will always be wholesome."

As soon as he arrived, Penn set his holy experiment in motion by telling the people who were already there that "Ye shall be governed by laws of your own making." But before they began making their own laws, he gave them a couple of his own in a document he called the "Great Law." Among other things, it provided for a three shilling fine or ten days in jail for participating in "such rude and riotous sports and practices as masques, revels, stage plays and such like."

But, more significantly, Penn's law said that "...no person shall be molested or prejudiced for his or her conscientious persuasion or practice. Nor shall he or she at any time be compelled to frequent or maintain any religious worship, place or ministry whatever, contrary to his or her mind...If any person shall abuse or deride any other for his or her different persuasion or practice in matters of religion, such person shall be looked upon as a disturber of the peace and be punished accordingly."

Other colonies had been established in North America long before Penn arrived and most of them professed to have religious freedom at the core of their belief. But Pennsylvania was the first that didn't reserve freedom for one religion to the exclusion of all others. And possibly even more revolutionary was the fact that Penn referred to the citizens of his colony in terms of "his or her." Some states don't seem to have got that message even now.

But while Penn was probably the most liberal of all the colonial proprietors, his liberalism did have some limits. He decreed that voters in Pennsylvania must be male and that men who voted must believe in God. He also ruled that to be a Governor, a member of the Assembly or a Councilman, a man must be a Christian.

Williams Penn's attitude toward the Indians was so enlightened that they called him "brother" almost immediately, and gave the same affection to the Governors who succeeded him.

Before arriving in America, Penn sent a letter to the Indians which he ended: "I am your loving friend." He seems to have meant it. He was well aware of how poorly the natives were being treated by the other American colonies and he believed, deeply, that they shouldn't simply be pushed aside just because an English King had given away their land. In a treaty with the Indians, Penn agreed to buy the land the King had given him and in the process set up a chain of peace that lasted well beyond his own death. Little by little, in exchange for blankets and hoes, fish hooks and kettles, he succeeded in buying all the territory the King had named Pennsylvania. In the bargain he bought peace and friendship that was unheard of in the other colonies.

But King Charles, meanwhile, was still busy giving land away and he wasn't being too careful about it. Penn had problems with Lord Baltimore to the south and with immigrants from Connecticut to the north. When someone told him that Philadelphia was the prettiest little town in Maryland, William Penn turned the other cheek. But when Lord Baltimore went to England in an attempt to prove that Philadelphia was on land that had been given to him, William Penn was forced to go back to London to defend himself.

He would return to America once again, but only for a brief visit. In all, William Penn lived in Pennsylvania for less than three years.

Much of his time abroad was spent encouraging immigration to his new colony. He knew that the key to success for his holy experiment lay in encouraging huge numbers of settlers. The first to be attracted were English, followed by large numbers of Welsh, who put their stamp on the Philadelphia area with place names like Radnor and Gwynedd, Penlyn and Bryn Athyn.

Penn traveled extensively in Germany and left a strong impression there. It was not surprising that they responded to his appeal. He told them of a territory bigger than Bavaria, Wurtemberg and Baden combined, and he promised them that they could live without war or persecution in Pennsylvania. The first of them settled in a place they called "Germantown," which became the first manufacturing center in the New World. The farmers who followed them spread the colony to the west into what we call "Pennsylvania Dutch Country" today. The name comes from the German's description of themselves as "Deutsch."

The Germans were followed by Scotch-Irish, the descendants of Scots who had settled in Northern Ireland. Others came from various parts of Europe to participate in Penn's experiment. Together they made it work. It was a rare combination, even for America, of people with strong traits that included thrift, industry, tenacity and an incredible desire for self-improvement. Coupled with Penn's ideas and the laws he devised to make them a reality, the Pennsylvania colony quickly became what all the others claimed to be, but what none of the others really were.

One thing America claimed to be, and undoubtedly was, was a melting pot. Pennsylvania could make the claim, but because of its rules that let a man or woman be anything he or she wanted to be, the melting process was cooled considerably. It's a tradition that allowed Pennsylvania Dutch country to come down to us in our time as a place that seems untouched by the trappings of 20th-century progress.

Members of the Society of Friends, the Quakers who started it all, seemed destined through the late 19th century to become an easily-recognizable group, obviously living in the distant past. In the mid-17th century, George Fox emerged as the leader of the Pennsylvania Quakers. His great belief was that his people should reject all worldly vanity. As a symbol of that rejection, men were required to dress in a style that was plainly out of fashion. At that time, well-dressed men wore detachable collars and fancy cuffs on their shirts. "Get rid of them," said Fox. Fashionable men were wearing narrow-brimmed hats with tapered crowns. The well-dressed Quaker looked for round crowns and broad brims.

They went around dressed like that until long after the Civil War. Then one day some smart Quaker asked another if it didn't seem a little foolish to have your clothes made for you at great expense, just to be out of style. After all, he reasoned, the idea was to show disdain for worldly things and here they were running off to expensive tailors for fittings. His reasoning prevailed and before the end of the century most Quakers were dressing just like every other American.

Another of George Fox's teachings was that no man was in need of any title other than "friend." He also believed that calling someone "you" was giving their ego too much of a boost. He began using the second person form, "thou" which, in the 17th century, was used to convey love. It was also used in worship, and, strangely, as a mark of contempt. The plural form, "thee" was, on the other hand, used as a sign of respect to an individual, and American Quakers began using the term "thee" as a general substitute for the word "you," either singular or plural.

Today's Quakers use their so-called Plain Speech only among themselves, but other sects in Pennsylvania have adopted speech patterns or, more to the point, have kept old ones that leave many of us scratching our heads. Take, for instance, the Pennsylvania Dutch woman who turned up one morning in the local drugstore. "What can I do for you?" asked the clerk. "Oh nothing," she said, "I just came in to go out." Or the farmer who killed a fox that had been terrorizing his henhouse. "Well, that's one more fox less," he said. Or the recent widow who explained that if her late husband "had lived until Monday, he'd be dead a month."

Visitors make pilgrimages to places like Kutztown in hopes of hearing people talk like that and they're often rewarded, if not a little confused. The people in Southeastern Pennsylvania we call the Pennsylvania Dutch trace their roots back to Germany and tenaciously hold fast to those roots. In Pennsylvania such things are possible. It has always been a haven for people who have brought strong ideas to America and never give them up. Sometimes, though, the ideas didn't quite work.

These days, California is considered a mecca for nonconformists and social experimenters. But they have a long way to go to match Pennsylvania's record for welcoming such people.

Sometimes, the dreams of the nonconformists actually worked. Evidence of one of the best of them is not far from Pittsburgh, in Butler County. It was the site of a model community established by a German immigrant named George Rapp in 1805.

Some people would call Rapp a communist today. Others would call him a genius. Before he arrived in the United States in 1803, he had founded a religious sect in Germany and, naturally, his followers were persecuted by their neighbors. He proposed to take them all to America and set out himself to find a place for them. He found a five-thousand acre site in Western Pennsylvania and sent word home that he had found a place with a future. But he cautioned his followers that it was in the middle of a wilderness and suggested that they might prefer to stay in Germany at least until the wilderness was tamed.

Six hundred ignored his warning. By the following summer they had cleared land and were at work building homes for themselves in a new town they called Harmony. It was agreed that no one could own property in the town and that the fruits of all labor belonged to everyone equally. The land had been bought for three dollars an acre with funds supplied by all the membership. Whatever they brought with them became the property of the entire community.

Rapp understood human nature and knew that such an arrangement wouldn't be everyone's cup of tea. Part of the agreement with each member allowed them to resign from the Harmony Society for any reason or for no reason at all. Anyone who did would be able to reclaim their original investment or, if they had come with nothing, would be reimbursed for the time and effort they had put in.

Within two years Harmony had enough grain to be able to supply other communities. They had wool to sell and were on their way to establishing a successful winery. They also had a profitable grist mill and shops that were patronized by people from miles around. Rapp believed in diversification and his ideas were making his community prosperous.

His followers obeyed his every wish. They never batted an eye the day he announced that sex was the undoing of Harmony and was, henceforth, forbidden. All marriages were dissolved and formerly married couples began living together as brothers and sisters.

It was no outburst of religious fanaticism, but rather Rapp's idea of sound business practice. People who have sex often have children and children represent extra mouths to feed. Not only that, but women with children didn't have as much time to work for the rest of the community. In another time and place, the Shakers tried such a rule and eventually vanished from the face of the earth because there was no new generation to replace them. But the Harmony Society was confident that new converts would take care of that problem. They were right, but in 1831 they discovered that converts can be a problem in themselves.

The original settlement was too far from outside markets to be as profitable as Rapp wanted it to be, so he packed up and moved his flock out to Indiana. They built a new town there that included factories and mills, even a distillery, and they prospered. But before long they came back to Pennsylvania and built another new town, closer to Pittsburgh this time, and they called it Economy. They did so well there that they attracted the eye of a German con man named Bernhart Mueller.

Mueller wrote a letter to Rapp from Germany which he signed "Count Maximillian de Leon." He wanted to become a Harmonist, he said, and he had forty followers who shared his goal. Rapp agreed and the stage was set.

The "Count" arrived in a lavish coach with liveried attendants. He was dressed in a gold-trimmed uniform with a heavy sword hanging at his side. For his part, Rapp provided the local band to give him and his followers a festive welcome to their new home.

It didn't take him long to begin a campaign to take over. He told the Harmonists that he had talked with God, who had appointed him to right some of the wrongs

they were suffering, not the least of which was to let them have a sex life again. In a matter of weeks he had swayed enough of them to present a petition to Rapp that made the Count the new head of the Society.

Rapp was able to fight him off, but the seeds had been planted. It was finally agreed that the Count's followers would be bought out if they agreed to leave by the end of the summer. Some 250 took the buyout and followed the Count down the Ohio River, where they set up a community of their own. Within a year they were bankrupt. The Count went back to Economy with a small army to get more money. But they were run out of town and the Count didn't stop running until he reached New Orleans, where he started another "ideal community."

Rapp's ideal community flourished for more than 50 years after he died and the Society became fabulously rich through investments ranging from railroads to oil wells. However, where there is money there are lawyers, and a string of lawsuits eventually brought the empire down right after the turn of the century. But the buildings they built, the graves they occupy, still exist in Western Pennsylvania.

The best monument to an American Utopia, and the best example of German architecture in the country, is at the other side of the state, at Ephrata in Lancaster County.

The monastic society that built and used the cloisters at Ephrata was founded in 1735 by Conrad Beissel, a man who has been described, alternately, as both a saint and a fanatic. Today we'd probably call him charismatic. Or insane. In Germany he had been a Presbyterian, but by the time he arrived in Pennsylvania he had become a First Day German Baptist, a society whose members are often referred to as Dunkers.

To say that his mind was inflamed is probably an

understatement. He was obsessed with finding out what the true word of God might be. After searching his soul, he concluded that the Dunkers had made a basic error and that the seventh day was the true sabbath. He published a tract on the subject and then immediately retired from the world, living in a cave that had formerly been occupied by a hermit. It took a long time before anyone could find him, and when they did his tract had won him a small band of converts. They rallied round him and, eventually, he told them he had been divinely inspired to gather them together into a monastic community. They built a meeting house and a convent and eventually had their own farms and factories. They established one of the first religious schools in the country and installed one of the best printing presses in the New World, which they used to print hymnbooks and devotional literature. They composed their own, strangely beautiful music, which is still performed today. And they earned the gratitude of their neighbors by helping out with big jobs on local farms.

Celibacy was one of Beissel's passions, but he didn't require it of his followers. Marriage was approved, but not encouraged. On the other hand, when he or his followers went out to preach in neighboring communities his message was instrumental in destroying many a marriage. It earned him a lot of animosity. But people who followed him were perfectly happy to accept living in tiny cells, with nothing more than a board to sleep on and a block of wood for a pillow. They seemed content to listen to his long, rambling sermons, even to listen to his singing. Up to a point, that is. According to one report, Beissel often preached with his eyes closed and sometimes opened them to find he was preaching to an empty room. But people said a lot of things about Paul Beissel. Many said he was a magician with awesome powers. He certainly had the power of imagination.

He convinced some of his followers that they could achieve a sort of immortality, a lifespan of 5,557 years, if they were willing to spend forty days and forty nights in seclusion, without a moment of sleep. Not just any, random, forty days would do, though; the sleepless nights had to begin with the full moon in the month of May. During the time, candidates would be required to live on bread crusts and whatever rain water accumulated. Early in the process, they would have to drink a special elixir which, they were warned, would make their teeth fall out and then begin to destroy their flesh. All would soon be restored, however, (if the candidate was worthy) and made new. At that point the seven Archangels would appear, to confirm the onset of immortality.

Many tried, but, as anyone who visits the Ephrata Cloisters today will tell you, there are no 300-year-old men wandering around on Mount Zion.

William Penn had said, "to be furious in religion is to be irreligiously religious." But he was true to his principles and made it possible for more than one hundred communities like Ephrata and Harmony to flourish in his colony. Not all the specialized communities were inspired by religious interpretations, however.

One of the most interesting of the entrepreneurs was a violinist who knew more about making a fiddle sing than about building a perfect town. But he worked hard at both. His name was Ole Bull. He was already famous when he came to the United States from his native Norway in 1843. Norway in those days was under the control of the Swedish King and Bull saw America as a perfect place to establish a refuge for his countrymen.

Ten years later he discovered Pennsylvania. He was convinced by a Philadelphia lawyer and a Williamsburg land speculator that the Shangri-La he was looking for was in North Central Pennsylvania. Bull went up to have a look and, sighing that it reminded him of Norway, he wrote a check to buy the land from the pair. It was hilly and rocky and covered with heavy forest, probably useless for farming, but Ole Bull was a dreamer, not a farmer.

The fiddler's plan was to mark off small farms which he would sell at cost to the folks back home. He would construct small towns, each with a church and a school so the Norwegians could learn English. To get the ball rolling, he went to New York and recruited a construction crew made up entirely of enthusiastic Scandinavians. With appropriate ceremony they began building a hotel and two dozen houses, plus a "castle" for Mr. Bull himself.

Part of the ceremony was the raising of a flag and the announcement that Ole Bull's first town would be named Oleana. With that, thirty-one cheers were raised, one for each state in the Union, followed by three more in honor of the musician who was orchestrating the whole adventure.

It was a huge success. Hundreds responded and trudged up to the back woods where four towns, Oleana, New Bergen, New Norway and Valhalla, had been built. But by the time he had finished building, Bull had run out of money. Then he discovered that, though he thought he had 120,000 acres of land, the actual amount was closer to 10,000. The speculator gave him his money back, but it wasn't enough to keep the community going and Ole Bull left Pennsylvania forever. He had brought eight hundred colonists into the state, but they dispersed behind him and all that's left of his bit of Norway in America is a memory of his unbounded enthusiasm in the form of the foundation walls of his castle overlooking the West Branch of the Susquehanna River.

Not far due East of Ole Bull's vision of Norway is a hillside overlooking the Susquehanna's North Branch that was once compared to France.

In 1793, a close friend of France's Louis XVI and a brother-in-law of the Marquis de Lafayette bought 2,400 acres in Northern Pennsylvania and began establishing a colony for refugees of the French Revolution. There were more than sixty houses there, which for a short time housed such people as Louis Phillipe, who later became King of the French, and the statesman Talleyrand. But at the center of it all was the largest log house ever built in North America, La Grande Maison. It was a three-story building, with sixteen fireplaces, large glass windows and wide porches. It was furnished with fine French furniture, and why not? It was intended to be the new home of Marie Antoinette, her daughter and the young Dauphin. They never made it. But the colony thrived as a haven for other aristocrats who were able to escape the French Revolution and who were joined by refugees from the French colonies in the West Indies, where slaves had taken advantage of the news from Paris to stage a little revolution of their own.

Other settlers in the area were mightily impressed, not only by the elegant houses but also by the elegant people in their midst. Many kept bits of lace handy to trim their buckskin when they went calling to join in the dancing and card playing or to visit one of the three taverns that graced the tiny community.

It all came to an abrupt end in 1802, when Napoleon announced that all was forgiven and that it was safe to go back to France. Many did; some others moved on to other parts of Pennsylvania. Within a year, the town they had called Asylum was deserted. All that's left of it today is part of the foundation of the great house they built to be fit for a Queen.

When land was being assembled to build Asylum, the sharp French pitted the existing landowners against each other in a scheme to keep the price low. Some of the original owners were from Pennsylvania, some others were Connecticut Yankees. The Connecticut men were told that the Pennsylvanian authorities were planning to take their land away from them; the

Pennsylvanians were told that people from Connecticut had valid titles to the land they thought they owned. Both factions were happy to sell to avoid what was happening a few miles down the river.

In 1742 the Moravian explorer Count Zinzendorf discovered a wide valley along the Susquehanna. It had been a favorite camping ground for the Delaware Indians, who called it, in their Algonquin language, *Maughwauwame*, which means "Big Plains." Settlers who followed Zinzendorf's directions shortened it and altered the pronunciation to make it Wyoming.

People who migrated north from Penn's colony based their right to settle on King Charles's grant of 1681. But nearly 80 years before that, King James I had given the Plymouth Company all the lands between the fortieth and forty-eighth parallels extending from the Atlantic to the Pacific Oceans. When some Massachusetts settlers moved south into the Connecticut River valley, the southern portion of the grant was assigned to them.

In 1750 some Connecticut people developed wanderlust and began heading west. When they crossed the Pocono Mountains and saw the Wyoming Valley they decided their wandering days were over. Like William Penn, they bought the place from the Indians, who never mentioned that they had already sold it to the white men from the south.

The first of the wars to settle it all lasted three years. As fast as the Pennsylvanians drove them out of the valley, new Yankee immigrants arrived to replace them. The Connecticut people won the first round. By 1774, the Connecticut Assembly had established the township of Westmoreland with 17 settlements along the Susquehanna, including Wilkes-Barre.

In 1782 the new American Congress ordered that the valley be turned over to the Pennsylvanians. With that the settlers burned Wilkes-Barre to the ground and the

second war began. It wasn't until 1800, after the New Englanders had decided to set up their own state, that the government in Connecticut signed a treaty giving the valley back to Pennsylvania.

It might all have happened sooner, but the Continental Congress had called for a truce in 1776. There was another war to be fought.

Though the first shots in the American Revolution were fired in far-off Massachusetts, the fire itself was started in Pennsylvania in 1774, when the First Continental Congress met in Philadelphia and sent a message to London that they were as much entitled to the rights of Englishmen as anyone in the British Isles.

After fighting actually began, the war became official at the State House in Philadelphia, known today as Independence Hall. The building had been home to the Pennsylvania Assembly since 1735. But in the spring of 1776, men like John Hancock and John Adams arrived from New England along with people like Patrick Henry and Thomas Jefferson of Virginia to assemble with Benjamin Franklin, Samuel Adams, George Washington and others to "assume among the powers of the earth, the separate and equal station to which the laws of nature and of nature's God entitle them."

Their first act, on June 15, was to name George Washington of Virginia general and commander-in-chief of the army. Within a week he was on his way to Boston to take command. The others stayed behind in Pennsylvania to begin establishing a new nation.

The Congress appointed Thomas Jefferson to draw up a document that would summarize their intentions and accompany their resolutions. He did the actual work in a house on the corner of Seventh and Market Streets in Philadelphia, about a block from today's Independence Mall. The result of his effort, the Declaration of Independence, was adopted on July 4. Very quickly, the

Pennsylvania Assembly ordered "that the Sheriff of Philadelphia read, and proclaim at the State House in the City of Philadelphia, on Monday, the eighth day of July at 12 o'clock at noon of the same day the Declaration of the Representatives of the United Colonies of America." As fast as word could travel, other Colonial Assemblies issued similar orders.

But the first reading, the most dramatic, was in Pennsylvania. John Adams wrote of the occasion, "Three cheers rended the welkin. The battalions paraded on the Common. The bells rang all day and almost all night; even the chimers of Christ Church chimed away." And of all the bells that rang that day, the loudest was the one that was hanging in the tower of the State House, the one we call the Liberty Bell today.

It had been installed there 25 years before to mark the anniversary of William Penn's historic Charter of Privileges. The bell had originally been cast in England, but the original cracked the first time it was rung. Two Pennsylvania craftsmen, Pass and Stowe, repaired it. They thought they had improved it, too, but the new combination of metals they used contained too much copper. For that, it was recorded that the poor fellows were "tiezed with the witticisms of the town." To save their reputations, they took the bell down and recast it a second time. And to put their reputation on the line, they removed the English foundry mark and replaced it with their own.

The bell stands in a special pavilion in Philadelphia today as a symbol of all America's liberty. In fact, the whole city of Philadelphia could be thought of as symbolic of American liberty. The ideas that won it were promulgated there because, in 1776, it was the largest city in Britain's American colonies, with a population of some 30,000. But the seeds of protest were planted there long before 1776. When the other colonies were indulging in little more than disorganized grumbling, Pennsylvanians were at work trying to change things. The principles of William Penn, the Quakers and the German settlers were opposed to going to war, but Pennsylvanians were very much in favor of standing up for basic rights.

In 1765 England decreed that the Colonials should help bear the cost of the French and Indian War by buying special stamps. The protest was heard up and down the Eastern Seaboard. It took shape in Pennsylvania in a resolution written by lawyer John Dickinson telling the King that Americans would not accept taxation without the consent of their legal representatives.

Parliament took Dickinson's petition seriously, or at least they seemed to, and repealed the Stamp Act the following year. But, a year later, the crafty politicians in London replaced it with a new, more lucrative tax on tea, lead and pigments for paint. They had already tweaked the Colonial nose by issuing a decree that all taxes must be paid in gold and silver, and not in the paper money issued by the Colonies. As the most important trading center, Pennsylvania became the center of protest over the new rules. It all prompted John Dickinson to start writing again.

He wrote a newspaper column called *Letters From a Pennsylvania Farmer* which were reprinted and distributed widely. Dickinson put into words what everybody else was thinking and his words became the rallying point for Sons of Liberty Societies up and down the coast.

In 1774, the revolutionary spirit came to a head in Pennsylvania when the Governor refused to ask the Assembly to deal with grievances against England. The people decided to deal with the matter themselves, and more than 8,000 turned out for a mass meeting aimed at either forcing the Governor to act or for the people to take the law into their own hands.

The meeting led to a formal convention attended by

representatives from all over the state which concluded that revolution was in the air and that Pennsylvania's destiny was tied to it, no matter what its formal government did or said. The Governor, William Penn's grandson, and a coalition of landowners and businessmen fought gallantly, but the events of 1776 put them on the losing side and a new State Constitution put an end to the old proprietorship that had begun five years short of a century before.

One of the prime movers was, after William Penn himself, possibly the most influential man ever to live in Pennsylvania. He was certainly the most interesting. His name was Benjamin Franklin.

He was born in Boston and migrated to Pennsylvania almost by accident. His first stop when he left home in 1723 was New York, where he had gone to seek his fortune. Having been a printer at home, his goal was the one and only print shop in New York. He should have written ahead. Not only was there no job available, there was no prospect of one. The proprietor of the shop suggested that he might do better in Philadelphia, a bigger city with more printers. And so the 17-year-old Franklin, down to his last dollar, decided to take a chance.

In his *Autobiography* Franklin described his arrival in his new home:

"I walked up the street, gazing about till near the market-house I met a boy with bread. I had made many a meal on bread, and, inquiring where he got it, I went immediately to the baker's he directed me to, in Second-Street, and asked for a biskit, intending such as we had in Boston; but they, it seems were not made in Philadelphia. Then I asked for a three-penny loaf, and was told they had none such. So not considering or knowing the difference of money, and the great cheapness nor the names of his bread, I bad him give me three-penny worth of any sort. He gave me, accordingly,

three great puffy rolls. I was surpriz'd at the quantity, but took it, and having no room in my pockets, walk'd off with a roll under each arm and eating the other. Thus I went up Market-Street as far as Fourth-Street, passing the door of Mr. Read, my future wife's father. When she, standing at the door, saw me, she thought I made, as I certainly did, a most awkward and ridiculous appearance. Then I turned and went down Chestnut-Street and part of Walnut-Street, eating my roll all the way. Coming round, I found myself again at Market-Street wharf, near the boat I came in, to which I went for a draught of river water; and, being filled with one of my rolls, gave the other two to a woman and her child that came down the river in the boat with us and were waiting to go further.

"Thus refreshed, I walked again up the street, which by this time had many cleanly-dressed people in it, who were all walking the same way. I joined them, and thereby was led to the great meeting-house of the Quakers near the market. I sat down among them and, after looking round awhile and hearing nothing said, being very drowsy thro' labor and want of rest the preceeding night, I fell fast asleep, and continued so till the meeting broke up, when one was kind enough to rouse me. This was, therefore, the first house I was in, or slept in, in Philadelphia."

That night Pennsylvania became his home. It became one of his passions, too.

At that time, Philadelphia was second in importance only to London in the entire British Empire. Franklin became intimately familiar with both cities. The day after his arrival in Pennsylvania, he found a job in a print shop. Within a year he was ready to go into business for himself and set sail for England to buy presses and type. He wasn't there long before his money ran out and he spent the next 18 months in London trying to raise more. He finally gave up and went back to Philadelphia and his old job. It wasn't long before he owned the place and became publisher of the *Pennsylvania Gazette*. Before long he started the *Philadelphische Zeitung*, the first newspaper published in the New World in any language other than English. Both were incredibly popular and hugely profitable. An ordinary man would have settled back and enjoyed his success.

But Benjamin Franklin was no ordinary man. He took a pen name, Richard Saunders, and began to publish an annual he called *Poor Richard's Almanack*.

"I endeavor'd to make it both entertaining and useful," he wrote, "and it accordingly came to be in such demand that I reap'd considerable profit from it, vending annually near ten thousand. And observing that it was generally read, scarce any neighborhood in the province being without it, I consider'd it as a proper vehicle for conveying instruction among the common people, who bought scarcely any other books. I therefore filled all the little spaces that occurr'd between the remarkable days in the calendar with proverbial sentences, chiefly such as inculcated industry and frugality as a means of procuring wealth and thereby securing virtue, it being more difficult for a man in want to act always honestly, as, to use here one of those proverbs, 'It is hard for an empty sack to stand upright'."

Franklin became a popular figure, indeed, around Philadelphia. It was only natural that he would get involved in public affairs. He began by establishing the city's first public library. Through it he was able to expand his own education, which had stopped when he left school to become an apprentice printer at the age of ten. His thirst for knowledge was immense and for years, he said, "reading was the only amusement I allowed myself."

His public career began to grow when he was elected Grand Master of the Pennsylvania Freemasons in 1734, 11 years after he first arrived in Philadelphia. Two years later he became clerk of the Pennsylvania Assembly. Not long after that he was made a justice of the peace and Deputy Postmaster of Philadelphia, a post that led to his appointment as Deputy Postmaster of all North America, an absolutely perfect job for a newspaper publisher who relied on the mail to distribute his product...and his influence.

Two decades later, he expanded his influence abroad. In 1757 he went to London again, this time as Colonial Agent for the Province of Pennsylvania. It was during his five years there that he took advantage of events at home to break the power of the Penn family and in the process became more powerful himself.

His influence expanded to the point that he became Colonial Agent for Georgia, New Jersey and Massachusetts. By the time the fight broke out between Britain and America, Benjamin Franklin was in the thick of it. He was on his way home from London, in fact, the day the first shots were fired at Lexington and Concord.

He arrived home to take his seat as a Pennsylvania representative in the Continental Congress and to sign the document it created, the Declaration of Independence. He lived long enough to also be a signer of the Constitution of the United States, which was also drafted in Philadelphia. Franklin was Governor of Pennsylvania by then.

Of all the men who set America on its course as a nation, only this Pennsylvanian, Benjamin Franklin, signed both the Declaration of Independence and the Constitution. He also signed the Treaty of Paris that ended the war with Great Britain and the treaty that had made France America's partner in the war.

Ironically, he wasn't in Pennsylvania during the war itself. He spent those years in Paris as the first Ambassador of the United States in a foreign country.

Franklin's accomplishments go well beyond his service to his country. Energy-conscious Americans are grateful to him today for the cast-iron stove he invented. The middle-aged among us wouldn't be able to read a thing without his bifocal glasses. And the big red barns that make the Pennsylvania landscape so charming possibly might not be there if they didn't have Franklin's lightning rods on their roofs.

But through his life he thought of himself as a printer and the epitaph he wrote for himself would lead future generations to think he did nothing else:

"The body of Benjamin Franklin, Printer (like the cover of an old book, its contents torn out and stripped of its lettering and gilding) lies here, food for worms," he wrote. "But the work shall not be lost, for it will (as he believed) appear once more, in a new and more elegant edition revised and corrected by the Author."

It's hard to imagine a more elegant edition of this amazing man. When he died, he left trust funds to both Philadelphia and Boston to help finance apprenticeships for young men under 25. "Good apprentices are most likely to make good citizens," he wrote in his will. The Philadelphia fund has grown to slightly less than a half-million dollars and is still being used to grant the loans Franklin requested. The trust will be dissolved in 1990 in accordance with Franklin's wishes and the money will then be divided equally between the Commonwealth of Pennsylvania and the City of Philadelphia.

Franklin became a very wealthy man, but not nearly as wealthy as Stephen Girard, his contemporary, who was rich enough to lend the United States Government $5 million to help it through the war of 1812. He made most of his money with a fleet of clipper ships that helped establish trade between the new country and the rest of the world, but he also dabbled in banking and invested in the new coal mines that would make many Pennsylvanians rich.

Though Girard didn't get involved in politics as Franklin had, he was very much involved in promoting the public good. In 1793, when everyone who could afford it, including Congress itself, left Philadelphia to escape a yellow fever epidemic, Girard stayed behind and took over management of the hospital. When he died he left his estate of $10 million to found a college to serve the needs of poor orphans.

But if Stephen Girard were to come back to Pennsylvania "in a more elegant edition revised and corrected by the Author," the Author would have an easy time of it. "Elegant" is a word that was never used to describe Stephen Girard. He didn't like to talk much and he didn't hear much of what was said to him because he was partly deaf. He was blind in one eye, too, and he didn't seem to care much what he looked like. One description says that he was wearing the same overcoat he brought with him in 1776 when he died in 1831. He never smiled much, either. But then, he didn't seem to have much to smile about. His only child died in infancy and his wife was hospitalized for 25 years of their marriage.

Girard had been dead less than four years when one of the great symbols of Pennsylvania wealth was born in Scotland. His parents were simple weavers whose business was lost in the Industrial Revolution. In 1848 they migrated to Allegheny, Pennsylvania where 13-year-old Andrew Carnegie went to work at his father's side for 12 hours a day in a cotton mill for $1.65 a week.

It wasn't long before he found another job as a messenger boy. All the great rags-to-riches stories of the period began with messenger boys, and this was one lad who was single-minded about trading his rags for riches. Less than two years later, he had gotten the traditional promotion to apprentice telegraph operator and in a move that would have made Benjamin Franklin proud, arrived on the job an hour early each day to make sure that he would learn the trade faster than the boys he was competing against. And when he wasn't learning telegraphy, he spent his time immersed in the Great Books, just as Franklin had done.

It wasn't long before he was on his way. He found a job as assistant to the superintendent of the Pennsylvania Railroad's Western Division. Six years later the superintendent was promoted and Carnegie took over his old job. There was no stopping him then.

One day he met T.T. Woodruff, the man who invented sleeping cars for railway trains. Woodruff was having trouble getting a railroad to use his invention and he told young Carnegie that if he could interest the Pennsylvania Railroad in it, he could have an eighth interest in the sleeping car company. Not long afterward, he acquired a large block of stock in the Keystone Bridge Company "in return for services rendered." The railroad was Keystone's biggest customer.

It wasn't long before Carnegie had to quit his railroad job because his investments were taking up all his time. "Nothing could be allowed to interfere with my business career," he said later.

By 1868 he was earning $50,000 a year. It was only the beginning. He graduated into the steel business and by 1900 his company's profits were $40 million a year and his company was the biggest producer of steel in the world. He was a legendary manager who operated on the theory that internal competition was good for a business. He goaded his supervisors into outdoing one another by taking advantage of their natural rivalries and jealousies. He did the same with his business partners. It was said that he was so good at keeping his people at each other's throats that some never spoke to each other for the rest of their lives. Quite a few never spoke to him after they left his payroll.

He was even tougher with the people who worked in his mills.

In 1892, workers in the Carnegie mill at Homestead went out on strike. After a month of negotiations, Carnegie's manager, Henry Clay Frick, tried a different approach. Three hundred Pinkerton guards were loaded on barges and towed up the Monongahela River from Pittsburgh. The strikers were ready for them and the river banks were lined on both sides with an angry reception committee. No one seems to remember who fired the first shot, but by the time the barges got to the plant gate, bullets were flying from every side. The tug boat that had towed them upriver turned right around to take the dead and wounded back to Pittsburgh, leaving the rest of the Pinkerton men stranded on the river in the barges, which became easy targets for burning oil, dynamite and rifle fire. When the smoke cleared a truce was called and the Pinkerton men were allowed to leave town by train.

A few days later, the Governor of Pennsylvania called out the National Guard and 8,000 armed men opened the Homestead mill on the company's terms. The terms were that the men who went back to work were not members of the striking union. They stayed off the job another four months before giving up.

It was the beginning of a management tactic known as a "lockout." It was a tactic that resulted in 53 major strikes in a single year in Pennsylvania alone.

But if such things suggest that Andrew Carnegie was a heartless tyrant, he spent his life trying to prove otherwise. When the Homestead strike erupted in violence, he was on an extended visit to Scotland. He never made a public speech nor wrote an article that didn't mention his high regard for the working man. But he seemed to be solidly in favor of the twelve-hour day and felt that the workers wages absorbed too much of the profit he could realize with improved technology.

If nothing else, Andrew Carnegie loved to make money. He also enjoyed giving it away. He spent millions building libraries, art galleries, music halls, building church organs, funding education, anything that would add to the general cultural uplift of the masses. He said that his own success and that of men like him was the result of foresight, resourcefulness and thrift combined with a general increase in population and community values. As a successful businessman, he felt that he had proven he was worthy of the wealth he had accumulated and to leave it behind for lesser persons to control was sinful. "The man who dies rich dies disgraced," he said.

But he didn't believe in charity, either. His money, he said, would be distributed to "stimulate the best and most aspiring poor of the community to further efforts for their own improvement." And he would be the one to decide what was most stimulating for his "poorer brethren" to benefit from his "superior wisdom, experience and ability to administer." He gave away so much money that he finally had to set up a foundation to do it for him. In the first half-century after he died, they gave away more than $200 million in his name.

If Carnegie didn't believe anyone was good enough to keep in his footsteps after his death, he wasn't looking around him for role models. He could have found evidence that inherited wealth can be put to good use in the sons and grandsons of Thomas Mellon, an Irish-born lawyer who later became Judge of the Allegheny County Court of Common Pleas.

Mellon arrived in Pittsburgh in 1834 to study law at Western University. The city had a university and a population of 25,000 by then, iron ore had been discovered nearby and there was plenty of coal to mill into five million tons of raw iron a year. But it was still a territory populated by hostile Indians. And the factories along the Monongahela and Allegheny Rivers had already covered it with a layer of soot. But it was a good place to be for a young man with ambition and Thomas Mellon had plenty of that. He had read Benjamin Franklin's *Autobiography* and decided to pattern his life on the principles of Poor Richard.

In a growing city, real estate was the way for a young lawyer to get ahead. Following Franklin's advice, Mellon invested every dime he could spare in loans that would help new arrivals find a place to settle down. When there are real estate investments, there are usually foreclosures and one big one pushed the Judge into the coal business. He eventually gave up the legal business, retired from the Bench and established a bank.

Then he carefully set out to raise his sons to make it grow into a prosperous future. The empire, guided principally by his son Andrew, who was United States Secretary of the Treasury under three Presidents, became involved in fields other than real estate, though their land holdings extended all the way to the Pacific Ocean. Andrew Mellon bought out a German coke-making firm and made it a major American industry. He also saw the future in aluminum and made Pittsburgh one of the world's leading producers of it. The family's holdings include such giants as the Pittsburgh-based Gulf Oil Corporation. In the late 1950s, when *Fortune* magazine identified the eight richest people in the United States, the list included four whose name was Mellon.

One of the earliest beginnings of the Mellon fortune can be traced back to 1845, when the City of Pittsburgh burned to the ground. Judge Mellon took advantage of the situation to get in on the building boom that followed. The Mayor of the city could very well have had him in mind when he went to the heart of the devastation, the point of land formed by the joining of the Allegheny and Monongahela Rivers and the forming of the Ohio River. "We shall make of this triangle of blackened ruins a golden triangle whose fame will endure as a priceless heritage," he proclaimed.

Many of his constituents couldn't help snickering, even though it was nice to hear words of encouragement. The low ground he was talking about was under water a great deal of the time. And if the ruins were blackened, the city had a reputation for being black and grimy long before the fire. A soldier who passed through there in the 1790s said "It's the muddiest place I ever was in. By reason of using so much coal the place is kept in so much smoke and dust as to affect the skin of its inhabitants."

They were right to laugh. At the turn of the century, Pittsburgh was known all over the country as "hell with the lid off." It wasn't until 1946 that a State park was begun on the Point after another fire destroyed an old railroad warehouse that was tarnishing its golden dream. With that, the city began to clean itself up and today it's hard for anyone breathing the air there to realize how heavily industrial Pittsburgh is.

It was George Washington who first recommended that the Point would be a perfect spot for a fort. He was a young surveyor then, out from Virginia exploring the possibilities of building settlements in Ohio. That Pennsylvania was key to the enterprise was proven when the French, who also had an eye on the Ohio Valley, took over the fort before the Virginians had a chance to finish it and built an even bigger one they called Fort Duquesne.

They blew it up in 1758 so it wouldn't fall into the hands of British troops who were closing in on them. When the British moved in, they rebuilt it and renamed it Fort Pitt, in honor of William Pitt, the English statesman. It was the largest British fort in America, but by the time the Revolution broke out it was in American hands. The problem was that the Americans were Virginians, not Pennsylvanians. Another border dispute was under way. It wasn't settled until 1782 when the Mason and

Dixon line, still the southern boundary of Pennsylvania, was made official.

Well into the 19th century, the city was an important center for Indian trade and as a stepping-off point to the wilder West. But as people went west, they began calling back for new shoes and saddles, knives and frying pans. Pittsburgh seemed like the perfect place to produce all those things and more. Then in mid-century the railroads came and the climate for business couldn't have been rosier.

The iron business, the coal business, the glass business were all thriving when the Civil War broke out. But they hadn't seen anything yet. By the time the war was over, the city was producing half the steel in the United States and a third of the glass. And when it was over, demand only increased. Men like Carnegie would profit hugely from the demand for steel to replace the wooden railroad bridges that were destroyed during the fighting.

Pittsburgh is the only city in the United States whose name ends with "burgh." In 1891 a decree went out from Washington that all "burghs" would henceforth be called "burgs." Pittsburghers didn't like that much and began to fight. It was a long and bitter battle that finally ended in 1911 when the name was restored.

Another Pennsylvania town that didn't have that problem is Gettysburg. They always spelled it that way. All its life, Gettysburg has been a quiet, pretty little college town. But on the afternoon of July 3, 1863, it became the scene of the heaviest artillery battle ever fought on the North American continent.

Two months earlier, the Union Army had been badly mauled at Chancellorsville, Virginia, and the Confederate Army had a new lease on life. They needed another smashing victory to get the financial support of foreign countries and their soldiers needed a boost in morale. Taking the war to Pennsylvania seemed a perfect way to do both. The two armies began marching northward in parallel lines. The Confederate General, Robert E. Lee, had the State Capital at Harrisburg as his objective. General George C. Meade, in charge of the Union forces, planned to engage Lee in Northern Maryland before he could cross the border, but he arrived too late. The Southern troops had gotten as far north into Pennsylvania as Carlisle and were studying the Harrisburg defenses by the time Meade sent a division north to find them. They found each other at Gettysburg.

The Federal troops were greatly outnumbered and retreated south to fortify themselves in a position known as Cemetery Ridge. Rather than attacking, the Confederates set up batteries and fortifications along a parallel ridge. The battle didn't begin until the following afternoon when Confederates attacked the Federal line. The battle raged for more than a full day and then the Union guns went silent after two hours of continuous barrage. General Lee decided that it was a sign they had run out of ammunition and ordered an infantry division under General George Pickett to charge across the meadow and storm the enemy's positions.

He had misread the silence. The guns opened up again and Pickett was forced to retreat in the face of awesome losses. Lee expected a counterattack, but it never came and on the fourth day he took advantage of a sudden rainstorm to begin a retreat through the mountains. The wagon train was 17 miles long and included some 10,000 animals, many of which were taken from Pennsylvania farms before the battle.

The retreat was successful, but the price was high for both sides. Of the 150,000 men who fought at Gettysburg there were 50,000 casualties. Before the end of the year, part of the site was designated a National military cemetery. On November 10, 1863, President Abraham Lincoln was on hand for its dedication, where he began a short speech with the words, "Four score and seven years ago, our fathers established upon this continent a new nation..."

Four score and *six* years before that day, the new nation was in deep trouble. In 1777 British troops had invaded Pennsylvania, defeating the Americans at the Battle of Brandywine and setting the stage for the fall of Philadelphia. Congress reconvened in Lancaster and after just one day decided to get themselves west of the Susquehanna River where it would be safer. They moved the country's capital to York, where America's first constitution, the Articles of Confederation, was drafted. York would remain the new nation's capital for the duration of the war.

Washington, meanwhile, moved his army from Philadelphia to nearby Whitemarsh. His plan was to use it as a base for an attack on the British at Germantown, but the plan failed when a dense fog rolled in before the battle could begin.

It was General Washington's darkest hour. He moved his army north to Valley Forge to wait out the winter.

One third of his army of 11,000 were sick, starving or worse. Washington stayed with them and pulled them through. "Naked and starving as they are," he said, "we cannot enough admire the incomparable patience and fidelity of the soldiery." Of the place where they wintered, a historian once wrote, "No spot on earth, not the Plains of Marathon, nor the passes of Sempach, nor the Place of the Bastille, nor the dikes of Holland, nor the moors of England, is so sacred in the history of the struggle for human liberty as Valley Forge."

Unless they take the time to study the restored buildings there, anyone who visits Valley Forge today might get the impression it's a nice place to spend a winter, a summer or an entire life. The gentle wooded hillsides sloping down to the Schuylkill River make it an unusually peaceful spot, beautiful in ways only Pennsylvania can be.

Washington's army spent part of the winter of 1776 in Pennsylvania, too, at a place William Penn described as the most beautiful landscape he had ever seen. It was "far ahead of anything that could be found in England," he wrote.

Washington had spent most of the summer and fall of '76 on the run and as winter set in, he stopped running a few miles north of William Penn's "beloved manor," his plantation at Pennsbury. It was the first relief Washington's army had seen in the whole war when they crossed the Delaware River into Pennsylvania. The General ordered that all the boats on the New Jersey side be removed so that the British troops, led by Lord Cornwallis, couldn't follow them. The plan worked and gave him time to develop a new plan. He commandeered every boat on the river and hid them out of sight. Then, on Christmas Day, he loaded 2,400 men into the boats and recrossed the freezing river. They marched to Trenton, New Jersey, where the British had set up their winter quarters and at dawn on the 26th, he made his first offensive attack of the war, easily defeating the Hessian mercenaries, many of whom were obviously suffering from post-Christmas hangovers.

The offensive began in one of the most popular visitor destinations, not to mention residential areas, on the United States East Coast, Bucks County, Pennsylvania.

People go there today to relax from the bustle of Philadelphia and New York. It's a short, easy trip from both cities, and that, in fact, is what put the Delaware River Valley on the map in the first place. In Colonial times it was a main stopping-off point on the York Road, the main highway connecting New York and Philadelphia. The early stagecoach stops, inns and

taverns made tourism the county's earliest industry and today the towns that sprang up around them are following in the tradition. But there was a period between then and now that changed Bucks County. And the change, as it happens, is part of its charm.

Towns that had provided lodging and ferry service for early travelers began to get industrial in the early 1700s when a grist mill was built on the present-day site of New Hope. It was followed quickly by a lumber mill, and the town was on its way. The location on the river made it easy to ship what they produced, but it wasn't perfect. In 1832, a canal was built parallel to the Delaware and for the rest of the century as many as 3,000 mule-drawn canal boats were traveling between Bristol and Easton, heading north with whiskey and coal and south with goods manufactured in Easton or imported through New York. As the largest town along the run, New Hope was the only place where four boats could pass at one time, and an outlet into the river made it the only point where boats could shuttle from the Delaware Division Canal on the Pennsylvania side to the Delaware and Raritan Canal across the river on the New Jersey side. It gave New Hope direct water access to New York via Princeton, New Brunswick and Newark Bay. The industrial boom lasted until 1931 when railroads replaced the canals and at that point, New Hope and the surrounding countryside became what it had been before; charming.

Fortunately for today's visitors, the canals weren't filled in, the inns weren't torn down. In fact, 60 miles of the canal's towpath have become a State Park as well as a National Historic Landmark and, especially in late September and October, it's hard to imagine a prettier place to take a walk or ride a bike.

Just about the time the industry in Bucks County faded, painters began arriving with bright colors on their palettes. By the 1920s, they had been joined by writers from New York and Philadelphia, sculptors, craftsmen and actors. It was inevitable that they would attract more people like themselves and would encourage local creative people to emulate them. It was just as inevitable that the old gristmill would be converted to a theater. It happened in 1939 and ever since, summer performances of Broadway hits, art shows, photography shows and crafts shops have been as much of a lure for visitors as the old inns and the canal towpath.

But as popular as Bucks County is, no county in Pennsylvania, or any other Eastern state, is as frequently a destination for tourists as Lancaster County, where people go to see the famous Pennsylvania Dutch. What they also see, and almost never fully appreciate, is the richest farmland east of the Mississippi River. That's one reason why the Mennonites, the Amish, the Dunkards and others settled there in the first place. It's a good reason why their grandchildren are still there. But the tourists aren't as impressed by the richness of the land as by the people who tend the beautiful farms. Their costumes range from the black dresses and bonnets worn by the Mennonite women, and the big black hats their husbands wear, to the plain homespun of the Amish.

But if the costumes are somber, the farms are far from it. The big red barns with their sloping ramps and high stone walls often become the strongest memory a visitor takes away. It's possibly because of the "hexerei" painted on their sides like some giant billboards. If you were to ask a dozen people what those hex signs mean, you'd probably get more than a dozen different answers. Most people seem to think they are meant to ward off lightning, a constant danger with big exposed buildings. But no self-respecting Lancaster County farmer would be without a weather vane that's been grounded and a set of Ben Franklin's newfangled lightning rods. Some say they keep witches away, and they do seem to do that. There has been no certified witch sighted in all of Pennsylvania in our lifetime. If they are intended to insure fertility in cattle, there is evidence that they may do the job in every pasture.

The big medallions often appear in groups of seven, which makes many believe that they are rooted in the Bible. Others say the symbolism goes back further to ancient cultures that worshipped the sun and the stars. Still others (cynics, to be sure) say that Pennsylvania Dutch hex signs are nothing more than devices to catch the eye of travelers who will then notice that the farmer has rugs and quilts to sell and his wife is offering homemade canned goods.

But whatever the Hexerei are trying to tell the spirits or humankind, the message gets through. They're like nothing else anywhere else, and have come to symbolize the Pennsylvania Dutch as much as poke bonnets and horse-drawn carriages.

Though Lancaster County had the first paved road in the United States, it never has been a place anyone would say has been overrun by modern civilization. The rich fields of wheat, corn and tobacco are tended in the same way they were three hundred years ago. The people have maintained the same language, the same customs and religion their grandfathers brought from Germany.

Their hospitality is legendary and their tables groan under loads of sauerkraut and shoofly pie, homemade bread and apple butter. Like the hex signs that symbolize them, the food they serve is unlike anything that's found anywhere else in the country.

They live by the book, and the most important book, after the Bible, is more often than not an almanac. Anyone who grew up near Manheim or Kutztown will tell you that cattle shouldn't be turned out in a new pasture except on a Thursday, which along with Tuesday is the most auspicious day to get married.

The almanacs that set down such rules vary from community to community, but the granddaddy of them all is *Johann Baer's Gemeinnutziger Pennsylvanische Calendar*. The Pennsylvania part of the title is a modern affectation. The original was written and published in Bavaria in 1476. It became an annual more than a century later, and another hundred years went by before a printer in Germantown began issuing it in the United States, where it was a best seller among the Pennsylvania Germans for forty years.

It told the farmers when to plant their corn, when to harvest their wheat, what to do in the rainy season. It told their wives how to make coleslaw and chow chow, how to get rid of a wart from their daughter's nose (not to mention how she probably got one in the first place), and how to ward off the evil eye. It gave them long-range weather forecasts, instructions on how to figure interest on a loan, and what to do about a debtor who might default on one.

It had cures for anything that might possibly ail you. If you had trouble sleeping, Baer recommended that you should repeatedly count up to two. No further, please. The trick was to exhale on the count of one and inhale on the count of two. It's easier than counting sheep. Earaches were easily cured by stuffing a piece of bacon a half-inch long into the offending ear. A cough could be stopped by drinking tea made from the leaves of a cherry tree, and the pain of a burn relieved by applying melted snow. Hoarhound tea would ward off the effects of snakebite, according to the almanac, and fried garlic held in place with a linen cloth would surely remove a corn.

The almanac was a recipe book, too, but it was sparse with details. One recipe for a cake neglected to tell you what to do after you mixed one pound of sugar, one pound of flour, eight eggs, a half pound of currants, one ground nutmeg and the same amount of cinnamon. The only other detail mentioned was to beat the egg whites for 20 minutes and the yolks for half an hour. By hand, of course.

Though every Pennsylvania Dutch farmer in the 18th century kept an almanac by his side, there were things the book couldn't do for them and there were always people ready to fill the gap. One such was a Lebanon preacher who became famous all over the Colonies for developing a cure for dog bites. He was so well-known that President Washington sent a servant down from New York to get his advice in writing. It wasn't all that complicated. The magic potion was an unspecified amount of dried pimpernel boiled in two quarts of beer then drained and mixed with two drams of theriaca. The mixture was to be drunk in pint doses, drunk without stopping to take a breath. Theriaca, by the way, in case you don't have any in your medicine cabinet, is a compound of drugs reduced with honey that our great grandfathers usually kept handy as an antidote for snake bites. It's also a fancy word for molasses.

Once the dog bite victim had drunk the potion, the cure wasn't complete until he had thrown away the clothes he was wearing at the time of the attack and had burned the straw the offending beast had used for a bed. It was also important not to eat the meat of a pig and to avoid beans, cabbage and peas as well as any creature that swims on the water.

The Pennsylvania Dutch often seem to live by strange rules, but their qualities of thrift and industry are rules that are the envy of us all. Though they are generally a closed community, occasionally one of them shows us what can happen when they apply their rules to the ones the rest of us live by.

Milton Hershey was such a man. His ancestors emigrated to Pennsylvania in 1717 from Switzerland where they had been members of a small sect known as the Swiss Brethren. When they came to America they became known as Mennonites, after their leader

Menno Simons. By the time Milton was born in 1857, the Mennonites were firmly established in the Lebanon Valley, but his father was a wanderer who seemed to fail at everything he tried. He ultimately went back to Pennsylvania, but his attempts at finding a career took him as far west as Denver. The son would profit from the failures.

Young Milton seemed headed for failure himself when he took a job in an ice cream store in Lancaster. His only duty was to keep turning the crank on the ice cream freezer, but he wasn't strong enough for it and the exasperated owner put him in the kitchen making candy.

He decided he had found his niche and before long went to Philadelphia where he sold candy on the streets during the day and manufactured it during the night. Probably because of lack of sleep more than anything else the little business failed miserably. Milton went west after that and got a taste of the real world for the first time away from the tight Mennonite community. He also learned a secret about candy-making, that real milk was an ingredient that made it better.

He took the recipe back to Pennsylvania and began manufacturing caramels. They loved them in Lancaster, but Milton Hershey seemed doomed to be unknown outside his own home town. Then one day an English tourist bought a bag of his candy and suggested that Milton ought to export his product. He had tried everything else and so it was easy advice for him to take. From that moment on he never failed again. In a short time he had to build a factory to keep up with the demand for his fresh milk caramels. America had not yet discovered chocolate. That happened at the Columbian Exposition in Chicago in 1893 and Milton Hershey happened to be there.

When he went home he began experimenting and quickly decided that his fellow Americans would beat a path to his door if he offered them a chocolate made with the same fresh milk that made his caramels better than others. He was right, of course, and in 1900 he sold his caramel factory for $1 million and used the money to finance a highly-automated chocolate factory near the town where he was born, Derry Church, Pennsylvania. It was a perfect site with good water and plenty of nearby dairy farms, but best of all it had Pennsylvania Dutch neighbors who he knew constituted a perfect labor supply, especially for a man like him who was one of them.

Hershey's chocolate factory was one of the first in America to be built where there was no town established. He remedied that by establishing one, which he named for himself. It is no ordinary town. As a Mennonite, Milton Hershey had a strong social conscience and he put the profits of his factory into making the town an ideal place to live. One of his first projects was a school for orphans, followed by an amusement park that would make them happy to be there. He built a golf course and swimming pools, theaters and playing fields for the people who worked in his plant. He paid for church buildings for any denomination that cared to establish itself in his town and he gave them a well-stocked library and a museum. It was a company town, to be sure, but it was the first company town that wasn't laid out with row after row of identical houses. It was, and still is, a nice place to visit.

To encourage visitors, he established a hotel on a hillside overlooking the town. It was patterned after a hotel on the Mediterranean, but it bears the owner's personal stamp. The lobby is modeled after a sugar plantation he owned near Havana, the dining room was designed to give sweeping views of the mountains behind it. As a well-known philanthropist, he had been asked to donate money to establish a national rose garden in Washington. Instead, he used his money to establish one outside his hotel. It is one of the biggest and most beautiful in the world.

Milton Hershey made chocoholics of us all. Another Pennsylvanian, Sam Kier, might take some of the credit for making our love affair with the automobile inevitable. Sam was a salt miner operating out of Pittsburgh. His source of supply was a few miles up the Allegheny River in a place the Seneca Indians had found some sticky black stuff bubbling out of the ground. People in the area had long since followed the Indian example and were using it to take the pain out of sore muscles. Sam took to bottling the stuff and selling it as "the most wonderful remedy ever discovered." He even wrote a poem about it:

"The beautiful balm from Nature's secret spring
The bloom of health and life to man will bring;
As from her depths this magic liquid flows
To calm our suffering and assuage our woes."

He may have been worried about possible lawsuits if anyone took his rock oil internally or he may have been just curious about what he was selling, but Sam took a bottle of his oil to a drug store to have it analyzed and discovered that if it were distilled, his Seneca Oil would be good for lamps. So he set up a distillery and went into the lamp oil business. It was the first oil refinery in the United States.

It wasn't long before Sam had competitors and Western Pennsylvania farmers were digging pits at the edge of their fields to encourage more of the black stuff to flow to the surface.

Then along came Edwin L. Drake. He had formed a company in his native Connecticut to explore the possibilities of forcing oil to the surface rather than waiting for it to trickle out and went to Pennsylvania armed with enough money to put his idea to the test. It wasn't easy. After months of trying, he finally succeeded on August 28, 1859. The world's first oil well, in Titusville, Pennsylvania, brought a boom to Western Pennsylvania that rivaled the gold rush to California

ten years earlier. The town of Titusville, which was home to less than 250 people when Drake's well began producing, grew to a population of over 6,000 in five years. New towns sprang up and disappeared just as quickly. Fortunes were made and lost, but the biggest fortune of all was made by an Ohioan who came across the border and took command of the entire industry, a young man named John D. Rockefeller.

Pennsylvania crude oil isn't used too much in the refining of gasoline any more; its quality as a lubricant is too valuable for that. But what if Sam Kier hadn't bothered to have the oil analyzed in the first place and people believed all it was good for was to calm our suffering and assuage our woes? What if someone had experimented with a different fuel for the internal combustion engine? Coal, for instance.

If that had happened, Pennsylvania would have been in the thick of the action anyway. Even before the Revolutionary War, both hard and soft coal were being pulled out of the Pennsylvania earth. When he was surveying the territory, young George Washington saw a soft coal pit near Connellsville and as early as 1760 it was being burned at Fort Pitt to keep the soldiers warm.

The Connecticut Yankees who crossed into the Wyoming Valley in the Northeastern part of the state found outcroppings of anthracite there but, like the Indians before them, had no idea what the black rocks might be good for except to amuse children who liked to look for the subtle rainbow colors that makes a piece of hard coal something more than just a black rock.

It was more than a dozen years after they settled there before someone decided that it might be useful as a fuel. They loaded some on a barge and floated it down to Philadelphia, but nobody there was interested in buying it. The industry went dormant until after the turn of the 19th century, when a Wilkes-Barre tavern owner built a grate that made it practical as a heating fuel. At about the same time the owners of a nail factory near Philadelphia discovered it was a good commercial fuel, too. But they weren't out of the woods yet.

Smart operators bought land with coal under it, but it took smart operators to sell it. They put coal stoves in taverns, hotel lobbies, anywhere people might gather. They hired people to keep the fires burning and in their spare time to teach people how to do it for themselves. It beat chopping wood, but it took the idea another decade to really catch fire. But by 1828, Philadelphia alone burned more than 77,000 tons of the black rocks and special canals were speeding more southward through the Lehigh Valley. At the peak, in the 1920s, Pennsylvania was producing well over 87 million tons of hard coal a year. At the same time, the soft coal fields yielded more than 135 million tons a year to keep the iron and steel mills glowing and to fuel the great steam trains, which seemed to be getting bigger and more powerful every year.

Pennsylvania hitched its wagon to the railroads right from the start. The first one ever built in America was a wooden-railed affair in a quarry not far from Philadelphia. In 1827, a nine-mile stretch of track was built at Mauch Chunk to reach the coal mines in the nearby mountains. It was not only the longest railroad in America, it was the country's only line powered by gravity. A steam engine hauled the cars up the hill where they were loaded and cut loose to race through a series of switchbacks downhill to reach the Lehigh Canal. It was taken out of service in 1870, but was quickly reincarnated by a smart promoter as a "scenic railway." For the next 60 years people lined up to be hauled to the summit and then raced downhill to the valley below. It was the world's first roller coaster.

One of the great pioneers of railroading, John Stevens, planned the country's first major rail line, an 81-mile stretch between Philadelphia and Columbia. When it opened in 1834, it made the trip to Pittsburgh one of the world's great adventures. Passengers boarded special coaches at designated Philadelphia street corners. The horse-drawn cars came together in Fairmount Park where they were hauled by a steam engine to the top of a hill. The coaches were fitted with an extra set of flanged wheels which were lowered at that point to engage with the road's iron rails and then they were hooked together behind a team of horses. They were ready to begin the first phase of the trip, 81 miles in ten hours.

At the end of the line in Columbia, passengers were shifted to canal boats for a trip along the Pennsylvania Canal, the Susquehanna and Juniata Rivers to Hollidaysburg, about 175 miles away. The trip would involve passing through 108 different locks. At the end of that leg, they were loaded back into railway coaches that were hauled up to the top of the Allegheny Mountains and then down the other side to Johnstown where another canal took them the rest of the way. The whole trip took four days. But it was a big distance; 394 miles. The system of canals and iron rails was Pennsylvania's answer to New York's Erie Canal which was making New York City the gateway to the West.

John Stevens, meanwhile, kept experimenting to give Pennsylvania the edge. A Pennsylvania inventor named John Fitch had developed a practical steam engine that could power a boat and Stevens reasoned that the same contraption could replace the horses that pulled his trains. Once he proved that it could, it was only a matter of time before his rail line to Columbia would be extended all the way to Pittsburgh, eliminating the canals. The time came in 1852 when he got a charter to establish the Pennsylvania Railroad. The canals had seen their day, and another Pennsylvania industry, the sturdy Conestoga wagons that had taken the country west, vanished completely. Not everyone was pleased. All over Lancaster County, where the prairie schooners had been a big business for more than a century, people were nodding gravely in agreement with a teamster's song that included the line,

"...May the devil catch the man that invented the plan,
For it ruined us wagoners and every other man."

But the railroad didn't ruin Pennsylvania. On the contrary, it expanded her borders. By mid-century, the Lehigh Valley, the Reading, the Erie and Cumberland Railroads were providing fast service for people as well as commercial freight into every state bordering on Pennsylvania, connecting all the major cities in the country. By the turn of the century, there were 60 major railroads moving across the Pennsylvania landscape. The sixty-first never heard a train whistle.

If New York had been first with a better canal, Commodore Vanderbilt's New York Central Railroad was determined to meet and beat the competition to the south. Vanderbilt had a line running west along roughly the same route followed by the old Erie Canal, but routes across Pennsylvania were more efficient and threatened to become more profitable. The Commodore, determined to get his share, began to lay out a route across Pennsylvania that would tunnel under the high Allegheny Mountains. He never actually built the line, but in 1883 when the Pennsylvania Railroad began operating along New York's Hudson River directly opposite his own line, the Commodore's son and heir dusted off the old surveyor's maps and sent a crew of 2,500 workers to dig the tunnels, build the bridges and prepare the rights of way. Two years later the two railroads agreed not to disagree and not to invade each other's territory. Six miles of tunnel had been built and more than 100 miles of roadbed prepared when Vanderbilt called off his men. It was beginning to look like Mother Nature would completely reclaim it when in 1938 someone convinced the State Legislature that they had a good head start on a super highway. Two years and $70 million later, Vanderbilt's railroad became the Pennsylvania Turnpike, the first such toll road, and still

the most beautiful, in the United States. By that point, Pennsylvania already had three times as many highways per square mile as any other state in the Union.

Which of Pennsylvania's highways is the most beautiful? That, of course, depends on whom you're talking to. It also depends on what time of year you're talking about. In the fall, one of the most breathtaking ways to enter Pennsylvania is along Route 80 as the Interstate winds its way through the Delaware Water Gap.

It's especially impressive for first-timers who have never seen it before nor heard that the local folks have always called the spot where the Delaware River flows between two peaks of the Kittatinny Mountains "the eighth wonder of the world." It isn't. It may not even be among the top ten mountain views in the world. But there is something special about it, not the least of which that it's a major gateway to Pennsylvania, and to Pennsylvania's Pocono Mountains.

It's also a direct route to Stroudsburg, one of the most charming little towns in a state that has more of them than any other. It was founded by Colonel Jacob Stroud, son of Sir William Stroud who, as a member of England's House of Commons, was the first influential man in history to try to ban smoking. In 1621, he told Parliament that "tobacco must be banished from the Kingdom and not be brought in from any port nor used among us." His proposal didn't get anywhere and he left England for America, where he invested in land at the edge of the Pocono Mountains that his son would turn into a thriving town.

Though the entire area thrives, it is among the wildest spots in Eastern Pennsylvania, where black bear still roam on some of the high hills and huge resort complexes with ski lifts and golf courses still manage to conceal themselves in thick forests. The average summer temperature in the plateaus on top of the Poconos is about 65 degrees, which makes the area a great place to escape summer heat, but not so terrific for farming. Probably because the mountains stretch off into the distance with no prominent peaks and valleys that make other mountain ranges more interesting to look at, the Poconos were slow to develop as a tourist spot. A lot of tourists liked that idea, and still do. It means they can explore crystal clear lakes and sit by roaring waterfalls often feeling completely alone in the world.

Some smart resort owners took advantage of that and promoted their hotels as perfect places for a honeymoon. They even added such things as heart-shaped beds and whirlpool baths in every room in case honeymooners might need added inspiration. But if you consider such things tacky, there are establishments in the Poconos to match any taste, from a charming complex of a 19th-century hotel and luxury housing at Buck Hill Falls to the ski resort at Split Rock Lodge.

One of the most charming of the Pocono inns is also one of the oldest, the inn at Swiftwater, which was established on the Easton-Belmont turnpike in 1792. Today it overlooks the main highway over the mountain and into Scranton, but at the end of the last century, it was well-known as the most fashionable hotel in the Poconos and the walk across the little footbridge that leads to its front door is as close as you're likely to come to taking a walk into the last century.

As though there weren't already enough beautiful lakes in the mountains, the Pennsylvania Power and Light Company made a new one in 1926 when it dammed the Wallenpaupack Creek and formed a lake that covers nine square miles and has a shoreline 52 miles long. It's named for the creek, but the locals call it "the Pack." The name is an Indian word that means "dead water," but the lake is anything but dead. The power company controls a 500-foot strip around it to allow them to raise and lower the water level to feed the three-mile flume that leads to their 40,000 kilowatt hydroelectric plant. Except for that, the entire lake, which is the biggest body of water inside the borders of the state, is available for having fun. It is stocked with fish, and its 14-mile length makes it terrific for all kinds of boating and water skiing.

During the last week in September, it's a good idea to head west through the Poconos, not because it's so beautiful in its fall colors, but that's the way to Bloomsburg and the great Bloomsburg Fair. It's not the only country fair in Pennsylvania at that time of year, but it is among the oldest. The first was held in 1855, and if you look closely at the most recent edition, you'll find things that may well have been there back in the beginning. They judge horses and oxen, swine, sheep and poultry with the same care today as back then. The farm machinery doesn't look the same, but the interest in it, reflected in longing looks, is just as strong.

What hasn't changed a bit is the hospitality, alive all year round in Bloomsburg. The people you meet are happy to be there, and happy you've joined them for a $3 turkey home-made by the ladies at one of a dozen local churches. They like the carnival rides and other commercial touches that have accumulated over the years, and they're glad to tell you the Fair keeps growing every year in a time when "growth" in other places often means moving away from the old ways. But everyone agrees that they hope it doesn't get *too* big.

The Bloomsburg Fair was a mature 21 years old when Pennsylvania staged one of the biggest fairs this country has seen before or since. It was built to celebrate America's hundredth birthday near the place where the country was born at Philadelphia. The Centennial Exposition was held in the 8,000-acre Fairmount Park, the biggest urban park in the United States.

The park had been laid out in the early 1800s and to bring it all together the city fathers called on Frederick Law Olmstead, who had earned a fine reputation as the designer of New York's Central Park. Olmstead took a look and turned down the job. "Nature herself has so adorned the space that little remains for art to do," he reported.

They hired a local man, Hermann Schwarzmann, to do the job and in 1876 a local poet wrote: "To fame a country's hundred years,/A camp of palaces appears."

Schwarzmann had taken on a big job. To build the camp of palaces he planted some 153 acres of lawn and flower beds, moved 2,000 trees and shrubs, built miles of streets, sidewalks and railroad tracks, not to mention several dozen bridges and fountains. In all they built 250 buildings to house the exhibitions, and, on May 10, 1876, all was ready for President Grant to open the Fair for business. A special Centennial March was written for the occasion by Richard Wagner, and John Greenleaf Whittier wrote the words to a hymn. And as the President ended his brief speech, an 800-voice choir sang the Hallelujah Chorus from Handel's *Messiah* while flags were hoisted up hundreds of flagpoles and 13 giant bells began to peal, competing with the boom of cannons firing a 100-gun salute. Then, as the band played *Hail Columbia*, a popular contender in those days to become the country's National Anthem, some 4,000 VIPs were escorted into the main building. What met their wondering eyes was the giant steam engine George Corliss had built to power all of the hundreds of machines on display in the Hall. It was truly the marvel of the age. The biggest engine ever built up to that point, it weighed 700 tons and could produce 2,520 horsepower with its two cylinders driving a 36-foot flywheel that revolved with nothing more than a whisper. The very sight of it made the crowd burst into cheers.

The cheering never stopped. By November, the daily average attendance reached more than 115,000. And before it ended, more than 8 million people had decided to spend the 50 cents admission to have a look at what America had accomplished in the short space of 100 years.

They saw a lot of steam engines and boilers, but they also got their first look at something called "internal combustion" engines powered by that new Pennsylvania product, gasoline. Some brewers showed them an amazing machine that would make it possible to manufacture beer without using any ice at all. Some day, they were told, the refrigeration unit would make the ice man obsolete. It was just one more thing that was too fantastic to be believed.

So fantastic no one at all believed it, was a small exhibit among the telegraphic equipment by a young inventor named Alexander Graham Bell. It was housed in the noisy building for two weeks before the judges got around to calling it "the greatest marvel hitherto achieved by the electric telegraph." There is no record that anyone else even noticed the telephone.

Photography was old stuff to Centennial visitors, but in the 37 years since the first pictures were taken, it was a field for professionals only. Now, wonder of wonders, manufacturers were showing pocket-sized cameras "finished in French walnut and ebony." For the first time, anybody with the price of a camera would be able to show off baby pictures around the office water cooler.

Drug stores hadn't yet gotten into the film processing business, but their business was well-represented at the Centennial, too. Drug manufacturers like John W. Wyeth of Philadelphia showed gelatin and sugar-coated pills for the first time. And one company proudly displayed an 800-ounce pyramid of pure morphine. Another Pennsylvanian, Samuel S. White, displayed the first false teeth made of porcelain "which will disarm suspicion of their artificial nature."

Americans saw toothpicks for the first time during that summer, too. And to beat the heat, they ate their first ice cream cones, often while taking a ride on the world's first monorail.

In the Women's Pavilion, they saw signs that the fair sex was going to have to be reckoned with one day, although some didn't seem to get the message. One foreign visitor wrote the folks back home, "...some individuals want to extend women's rights to unnatural and insane extremes." But he added, "It is unmistakable that the application of this great principle has importantly contributed to the development of the nation."

The exhibits in the Women's Pavilion ranged from a pair of linen napkins spun by the hand of Queen Victoria to a machine that had been invented by a woman to wash blankets. But the most popular exhibit there, and to many at the whole Fair, was a sculpture made of butter by an Arkansas housewife. Though Fair records called it "beautiful and unique," no one recorded what it smelled like by the time the Fair closed in November.

When the Fair closed with the touch of a telegraph key that stopped the Corliss Engine, exhibits were dismantled and the buildings torn down. A whole trainload of artifacts, in no less than 42 freight cars, was shipped to Washington and put on permanent display in the Smithsonian Institution's Arts and Industries Building. Many of the plants and shrubs were moved to nearby Longwood Gardens. The sculpture of an arm holding a torch, called the "Statue of Independence" by its sculptor Frederic Bartholdi, was moved to Madison Square Park in New York to wait for the rest of the figure, which would be placed in the harbor and renamed the Statue of Liberty. The mighty Corliss Engine was shipped off to Chicago to go to work in the Pullman railway car factory.

The Centennial gave Europe a much different view of America and, for the first time, Americans became known all over the world as "bold...powerful... energetic...big," and, most of all, "progressive." *The Times* of London said, "The New Englander (*sic*!) mechanizes as an old Greek sculptured, as the Venetian painted or the modern Italian sings. A school has grown up whose dominant quality, curiously intense, widespread and daring, is mechanical imagination."

They knew for the first time that America was the greatest industrial power in the world. And on their side of the Atlantic, Americans discovered confidence in themselves. Their roots were in Europe as children look at their parents. After the summer of 1876 they took a good look at themselves and they liked very much what they saw. Significantly, the window they looked through was no less a place than Pennsylvania.

(Previous page and bottom left) Benjamin Franklin Bridge, Philadelphia, spanning the Delaware River to Camden. (Left) City Hall, Penn Square. (Below) Dilworth Plaza. (Bottom right) the Liberty Bell, venerated symbol of freedom. (Facing page) Independence Hall, where the Constitution was written.

(Left) Elfreth's Alley, lined with 18th-century houses, is the oldest unchanged street in Philadelphia. (Top) Independence Hall. (Above) outside the Museum of Art. (Facing page) panoramic view of the historic city.

(These pages) the layout of Philadelphia was originally conceived by William Penn in 1682, making it the first planned city in the New World. It became the center of political control of the Colonies during the Revolutionary period, until occupied by the British in 1777.

(Facing page) the grandiose splendor of the Pennsylvania
Academy of Fine Arts. (Above) the Assembly Room of
Independence Hall in Philadelphia. Built in 1732, the Hall
has been faithfully restored to its appearance when the
Declaration of Independence was adopted there in 1776.

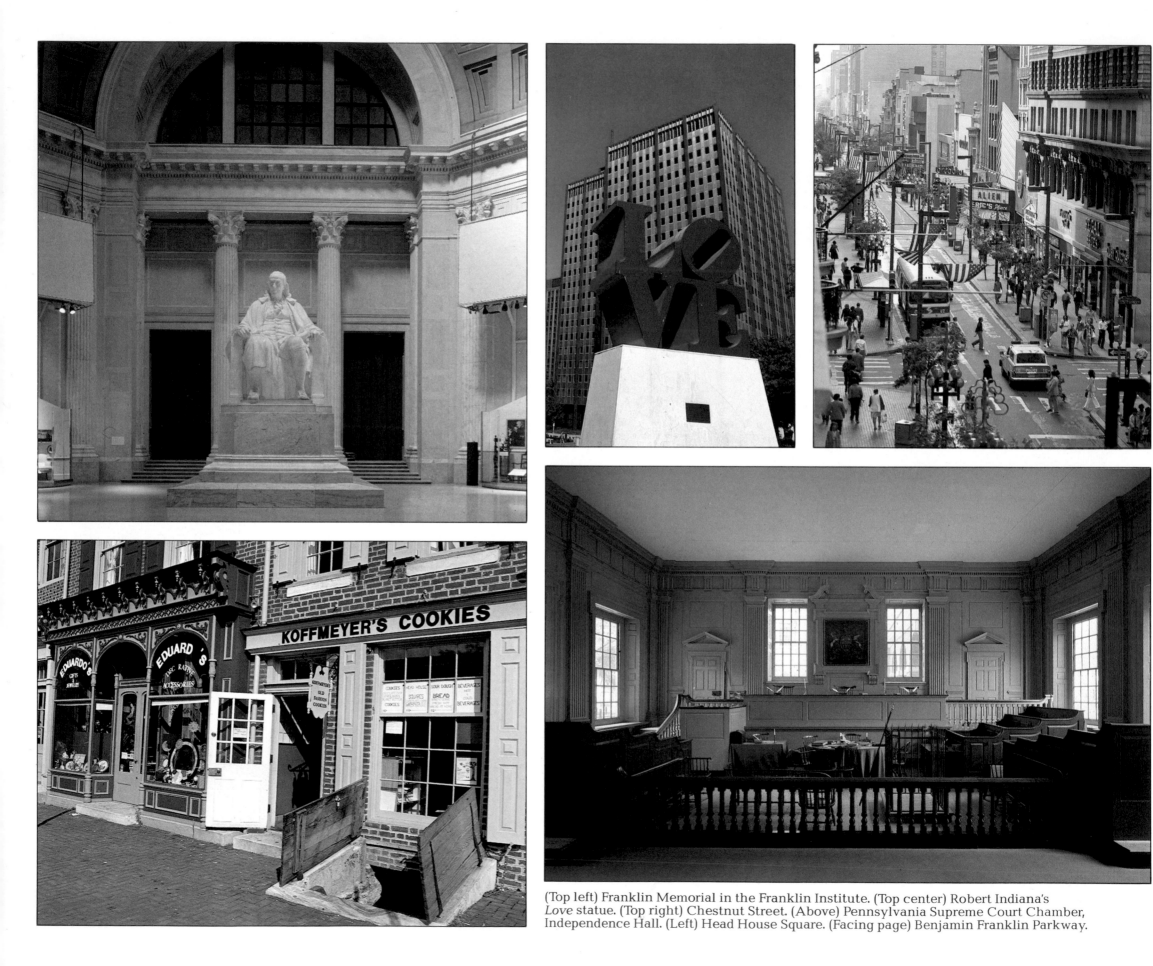

(Top left) Franklin Memorial in the Franklin Institute. (Top center) Robert Indiana's *Love* statue. (Top right) Chestnut Street. (Above) Pennsylvania Supreme Court Chamber, Independence Hall. (Left) Head House Square. (Facing page) Benjamin Franklin Parkway.

(Above) reconstructed huts at Valley Forge, where the troops of General George Washington were quartered during the terrible winter of 1777-78. He said, "To see men without clothes to cover their nakedness, without blankets to lie upon, without shoes...without a house or hut to cover them until those could be built, and submitting without a murmur, is a proof of patience and obedience which, in my opinion, can scarcely be paralleled" (December 23, 1777). Their endurance here in the face of great privation, which left over 2,000 soldiers dead, helped develop a spirit of resolve which they carried with them on June 19, 1778, when they left Valley Forge to pursue the British Army. (Left) the National Memorial Arch, which commemorates the "patience and fidelity" of the troops. (Far left) Washington's Headquarters. (Top left and facing page) cannon in the Artillery Park.

(Above) Brandywine Baptist Church. (Facing page) General
Lafayette's Headquarters, Brandywine Battlefield Park, where
the French marquis stayed before fighting with distinction
against the British, who were led by General Howe.

(These pages) inside the conservatories of Longwood
Gardens, which lie 30 miles west of Philadelphia in the
Brandywine Valley. This horticultural delight, covering 350
acres, was created by Pierre Samuel du Pont (1870-1954).

(Above) Ephrata Cloister was a radical religious and communal society founded in 1732 by Conrad Beissel. However, by 1800 the celibate group was practically extinct. (Facing page) Amish farm, Lancaster County.

(These pages) the Pennsylvania Farm Museum at Landis Valley recreates the atmosphere of rural life in the state from Colonial times to the end of the 19th century. (Top left) the Yellow Barn, Seamstress House and Tavern. (Top right) the Settler's Farm complex represents a German immigrant's farmstead. (Above) the Tavern captures the ambience of an early 19th-century country inn. (Right and facing page) the Landis House of 1870, furnished in Victorian style.

(These pages and overleaf) the Railroad Museum of Pennsylvania, Strasburg. (Above and top left) the bright yellow, open observation coach was featured in the film *Hello Dolly!*, starring Barbara Streisand. (Overleaf, left) steam locomotive seen from Carpenters Graveyard.

(These pages) Lancaster County's Amish country, where gentle pastoral and farming scenes delight the eye, and the fast pace of the 20th century seems a dream away. (Overleaf) no tractors, just animals whose "...hooves like pistons in an ancient mill / Move up and down, yet seem as standing still" (Edwin Muir).

(These pages and overleaf) in Amish country. (Above) horse-drawn buggy clip-clops briskly along the road, while cattle browse amidst the verdant landscape. (Facing page) tranquil farmhouse scene.

(These pages and overleaf) rural scenes in Amish country, where the "vanities" of the 20th century are scorned and travel is by horse and buggy (left). (Bottom left and bottom right) faithful animals tread a weary path, and the curtain of time is set aside as the share cuts the furrow into rutted lanes, as of yore.

(These pages) Harrisburg, the state capital. (Top right) the rotunda and (left) the entrance hall to the House of Representatives (facing page) in the Capitol Building, built in the Italian Renaissance style. (Top left) house on State Street. (Above) Strawberry Square shopping complex on Walnut Street.

(Above) the Maclay Mansion, Harrisburg. It was William
Maclay who laid out the settlement in 1785 for John Harris,
Jr., when it became known as Louisbourg instead of Harris'
Ferry. (Facing page) the dome of the Capitol Building.

B O A L S B U R G

AN AMERICAN VILLAGE ON THE NATIONAL HISTORIC REGISTER

BIRTHPLACE OF MEMORIAL DAY

THE CUSTOM OF DECORATING SOLDIERS' GRAVES WAS BE-
GUN HERE IN OCTOBER, 1864, BY EMMA HUNTER, SOPHIE
KELLER, AND ELIZABETH MYERS.

NAMED FOR DAVID BOAL WHO SETTLED HERE IN 1798.
VILLAGE LAID OUT IN 1808. BOALSBURG TAVERN BUILT 1819.
POST OFFICE ESTABLISHED 1820. FIRST CHURCH ERECTED 1827.
HOME COMMUNITY OF THREE UNITED STATES AMBASSADORS.

(Facing page) farm near State College, which was settled in 1859 and named after
Pennsylvania State College, now Pennsylvania State University. (This page)
Boalsburg, once an important stagecoach stop, was founded in 1810, and named
after its founder David Boal.

(Above) the Horseshoe Curve, Altoona – sweeping high through the Alleghenies – is a remarkable feat of engineering and was opened to rail traffic on February 15, 1854. (Facing page) an ornate bandstand at Ligonier.

(These pages) Pittsburgh. (Above) the downtown district
from Mount Washington. (Facing page) Point State Park,
formerly the site of several forts, lies at the strategic
confluence of the Allegheny, Monongahela and Ohio Rivers.

(Far left) Flag Plaza, site of the Boy Scouts of America Building.

(Left) the 42-story, Gothic-styled Cathedral of Learning, University of Pittsburgh.

(Bottom left) the Heinz Chapel on the University of Pittsburgh campus is notable for its gorgeous, 73-foot-high stained-glass windows.

(Below) Allegheny Observatory, in Riverview Park, houses a 116-foot telescope. The observatory was made responsible for the provision of accurate time in 1869. In 1881, the discovery of the infra-red spectrum in sunlight was made here and, in 1895, its astronomers were able to show that Saturn's rings are made up of individual particles. The discovery that stars rotate on their own axes in the same manner as planets was made here in 1909.

(Facing page) Allegheny County Soldiers' Memorial.

(Overleaf) Pittsburgh at night, as seen from Mount Washington.

(These pages) Kennywood Park, where people can enjoy the colorful amusement rides, which include four roller coasters, as well as Kiddieland, a swimming pool and a picnic area. (Overleaf) stern-wheelers of the Gateway Clipper Fleet plying the turbid waters of the Monongahela River: (left) the *Good Ship Lollipop* and (right) the *Liberty Belle*.

(Left) Allegheny Center Mall. (Bottom left) at North Shore Center, looking across the Allegheny River. (Bottom right) Station Square and a Bessemer converter, which forms part of an outdoor museum. (Below) the stern-wheeler *Liberty Belle*. (Facing page and overleaf) Pittsburgh seen from Mount Washington.

(Below and bottom left) the high-rise city skyline seen from Station Square. (Bottom right) the stern-wheeler *Good Ship Lollipop* drives its way along the Monongahela River. (Left and facing page) Pittsburgh as viewed from Mount Washington.

(These pages) Pittsburgh. (Overleaf, top left) Pittsburgh
National Bank. (Top center) U.S. Steel Building. (Top right and
facing page) the Gateway Center. (Bottom left and bottom right)
P.P.G. Place Plaza. (Bottom center) Smithfield Bridge.

(These pages) Pittsburgh, the "City of Bridges". (Top left) spanning the Monongahela River. (Top right) Fort Pitt Bridge. (Above and left) Three Rivers Stadium. (Facing page) crossing the Allegheny River above Point State Park are Fort Duquesne, 6th Street, 7th Street, 9th Street, Ft. Wayne Railroad and 16th Street Bridges.

(Left) memorial at the site of Fort Le Boeuf, where George Washington came in 1753 as an envoy of the Governor of Virginia. (Above) the Judson House of 1820, Fort Le Boeuf. (Top) Drake Well Museum, Titusville, where the world's first oil well was drilled in 1859. (Facing page) Conneaut Lake, west of Meadville.

(Left) State Street, Erie. (Bottom left) boy fishing and (bottom right and below) the beach at Presque Isle. In 1813, at Presque Isle Bay, Oliver Hazard Perry constructed the ships which engaged the British in the Battle of Lake Erie. (Facing page) sunset over Lake Erie. (Overleaf) Pennsylvania's Grand Canyon.

(Above, top left and top right) Pine Creek, near Jersey Mills; a likely spot for fishermen to catch brown or rainbow trout, or the native brookies. (Right and facing page) spectacular views from the rim of Pennsylvania's Grand Canyon.

(Above) sun-dappled scene within Colton Point State Park. (Facing page, top left) North Bend U.M. Church. (Top right) Wellsboro. (Bottom left) covered bridge near Bloomsburg. (Bottom right) old house near Hyner. (Overleaf, left) at Loganton. (Overleaf, right) covered bridge at Washingtonville.

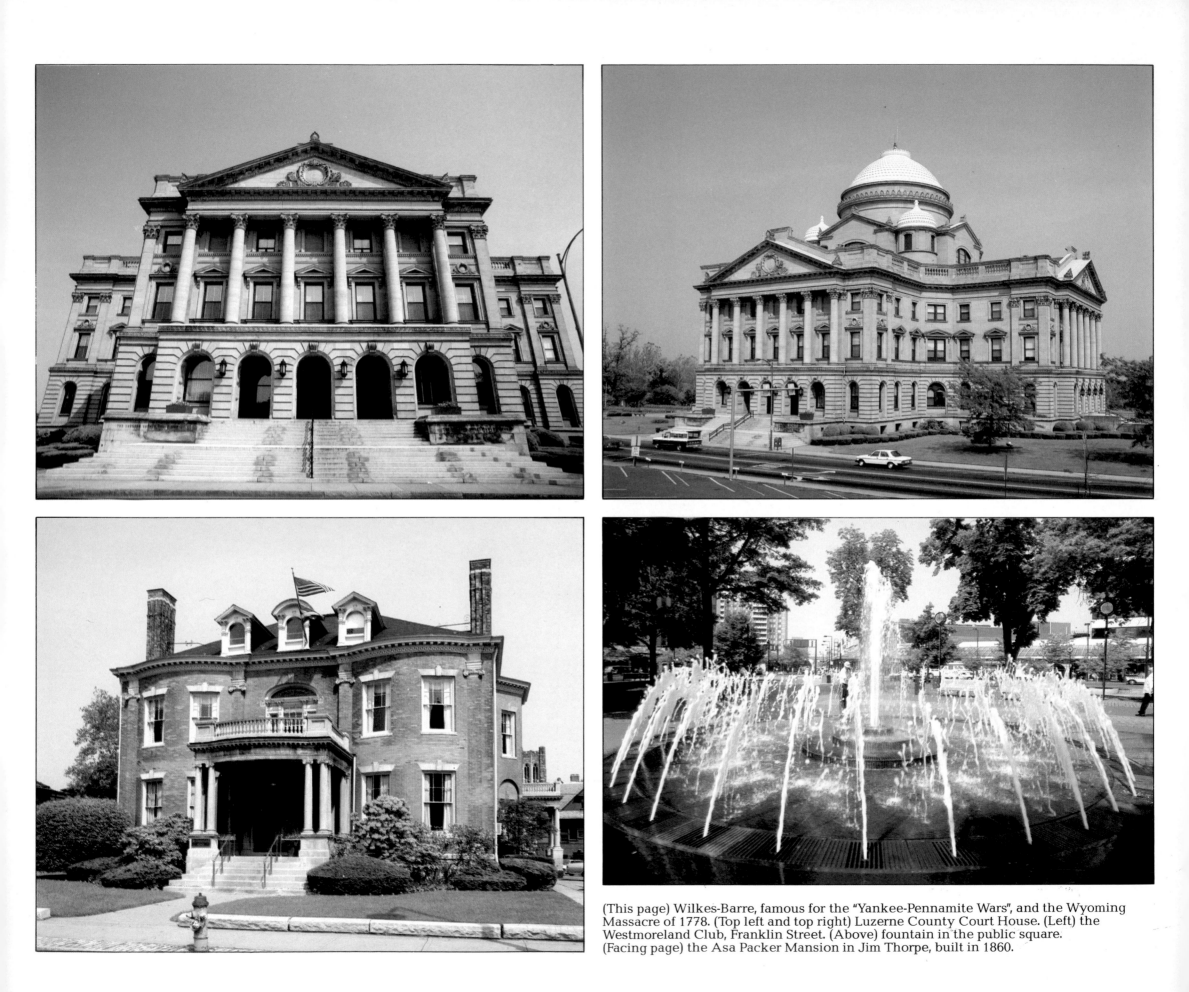

(This page) Wilkes-Barre, famous for the "Yankee-Pennamite Wars", and the Wyoming Massacre of 1778. (Top left and top right) Luzerne County Court House. (Left) the Westmoreland Club, Franklin Street. (Above) fountain in the public square. (Facing page) the Asa Packer Mansion in Jim Thorpe, built in 1860.

(Above) Route 315 into Wilkes-Barre. (Facing page) Main
Street, Jim Thorpe. (Overleaf) views from Camelback
Mountain, Big Pocono State Park, Tannersville. Camelback
forms the center of a popular ski resort.

(Top left) Pine Crest Yacht Club, Lake Wallenpaupack. (Left) sign for the Delaware Water Gap National Recreation Area. (Above) Jim Thorpe. (Top right) Main Falls and (facing page and overleaf) Upper Canyon Falls at Bushkill Falls, which were first opened to the public by Charles E. Peters in 1904.

(Above) the Scranton Iron Furnaces, built between 1841 and 1857, used anthracite for fuel. (Remaining pictures) Eckley Miners' Village, eight miles east of Hazelton, is a recreation of a 19th-century anthracite mining community.

(Far left) interior of the Zion Reformed Church, Allentown. When in 1777, after the Battle of Brandywine, it became obvious to George Washington that the British would occupy Philadelphia, the Liberty Bell and the bells of Christ Church were temporarily removed to Allentown and hidden in the Zion Reformed Church.
(Below) interior of the Liberty Bell Shrine under the Zion Reformed Church. The exact replica of the bell is in the position where the original was placed.
(Bottom left) Lehigh County Court House, Hamilton Mall.
(Left) the Old Court House.
(Facing page) Trout Hall, Allentown, was built in 1770 by the son of the city's founder – Chief Justice William Allen. The mansion was named after the justice's hunting lodge. (Top left) the Master Bedroom. (Top right) view of the exterior. (Bottom right) the Empire Room. (Bottom left) the Great Hall.

(These pages) Bethlehem, where Moravian immigrants settled in 1741. (Above) interior of the Central Moravian Church of 1806. (Facing page) tree-lined path near the church. (Top left) the Bell House. (Top right) East 4th Street. (Right) the Moravian Museum, originally the *Gemeinhaus* or Community House.

(Bottom left) Washington Crossing, where on Christmas night 1776, George Washington crossed the Delaware River to attack at Trenton. (Below) New Hope. (Right) the Parry Mansion, built in 1784 by local mill owner Benjamin Parry. (Bottom right and facing page) mule-drawn barge rides on the Old Delaware Canal.

(Left) Moravian Pottery and Tile Works, Doylestown. (Bottom left and facing page) the Mercer Museum houses a large collection of preindustrial equipment, tools and other interesting items. (Below, bottom right and overleaf) the beautiful National Shrine of Our Lady of Czestochowa, near Doylestown.

(These pages) the ornate Fonthill Museum, Doylestown, was
built by Dr. Henry Chapman Mercer and contains world-famous
examples of tilework, as well as many fine engravings and
prints.

(Left) Stagecoach Tavern, Historic Fallsington. (Top left) bridge over the Delaware River near Lumberville. (Top right) Thompson-Neely House, in Washington Crossing Historic Park, where it is believed that George Washington and his officers planned the Battle of Trenton. (Above) statue of Washington crossing the Delaware. (Facing page) Pennsbury Manor, the reconstructed home of William Penn.

(Previous pages) views of the battlefield of Gettysburg from the Observation Tower. (Facing page) the Pennsylvania Memorial. (Top left) stone markers indicate the resting places of Union dead. (Top right) the Minnesota and Pennsylvania Memorials. (Above) Cemetery Hill. (Right) Gettysburg Cemetery and the Observation Tower. (Overleaf) statuary on Cemetery Ridge.

(These pages) scenes at Gettysburg, where the tide of the Confederate advance was bloodily broken. (Top center) the site where Abraham Lincoln made the Gettysburg Address on November 19, 1863: "Four score and seven years ago our fathers brought forth on this continent a new nation, conceived in Liberty..."

(Previous pages) Cemetery Ridge. (Bottom left) farm near Gettysburg. (Facing page) the Headquarters of the Army of the Potomac. (Remaining pictures and following pages) artillery pieces now lie silent on the Gettysburg battlefield, though once they thundered with the loud-mouthed voice of war.